Villain Academy

by Sam Hay

Illustrated by Bill Ledger

OXFORD

UNIVERSITY PRESS

In this story ...

Ben
(Sprint)

Ben is super fast! He can run faster than a racing car. Once, he ran five times round the school grounds in under ten seconds.

Pip
(Boost)

Axel
(Invisiboy)

Mrs Butterworth
(cook)

The Head
(head teacher)

Chapter 1:
Running to the future

Ben put down his book and rubbed his eyes. "My head hurts," he told Pip. "Gadget-safety, costumes through the ages ... I'll never remember it all."

Pip smiled. "Keep studying, Ben. There's still an hour before our last HAT."

The Hero Academy Tests

The Hero Academy Tests (HATs) are taken at the end of each year. They are an opportunity for the heroes to show what they have learned.

Ben's favourite test:
Name that villain.
The heroes are given a series of clues, and they have to identify the villain.

Pip's toughest test:
Make your own superhero costume.
(Pip can't stand sewing!)

After the tests are over, the heroes are all given special hats to wear for the HATs awards ceremony.

"Big news!" cried Axel, rushing into the library.
"Shh!" said Pip. "We're revising for the HAT."
"But look," Axel whispered, showing them his tablet.

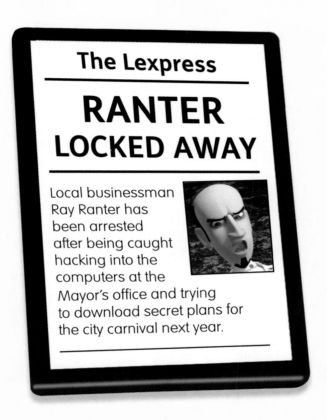

The Lexpress

RANTER
LOCKED AWAY

Local businessman Ray Ranter has been arrested after being caught hacking into the computers at the Mayor's office and trying to download secret plans for the city carnival next year.

"Told you it was big news!" Axel said with a grin. "The biggest villain in Lexis City is behind bars."

Just then, Slink, the school cat, came in and meowed. He started to paw at Ben's shoes.

"I think he wants you to follow him," Pip said.

Ben followed Slink to the Head's office. He went inside, his heart beating fast. Whatever the Head wanted him for, it had to be important.

"Ben," said the Head gravely. "Hero Academy is in danger. Only you can save us from Ray Ranter."

Ben gasped. "But Ray Ranter is in jail!"

The Head nodded. "He is for now. The danger we face is in the future. My supercomputer brain predicts a 99% chance that Ray Ranter will escape and take over Hero Academy next term."

"What? We must never let that happen!" Ben cried fiercely. "How do we stop him?"

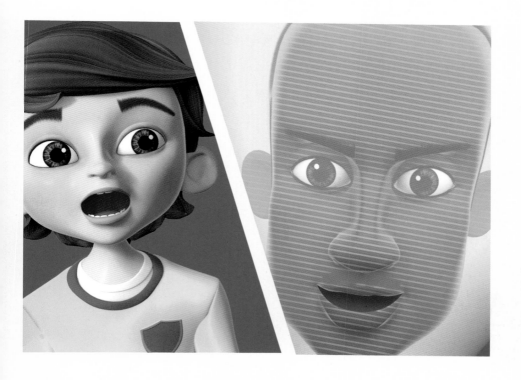

"You must travel to the future," said the Head. Ben's jaw dropped. "The future? How?"
The Head smiled. "By using the Treadmill Time Machine."

The Head looked towards the far corner of his office. Ben followed his gaze and saw a running machine.

"It's an invention that Mrs Molten has just finished," the Head explained.

The machine had a control panel. On it were the words: THE PRESENT.

"If you run forwards, you will travel into the future," the Head explained. "Running backwards will send you into the past. Only you can run fast enough to use it, Ben."

Ben stepped on the machine. It switched on with a hum. Very slowly, the treadmill began to move. At first, Ben walked to keep up with it. Then, gradually, he had to increase his speed to jogging pace.

"Run, Ben," said the Head. "Run faster than you've ever run before. I may not be there to help you in the future, but you must find a way to save Hero Academy from Ray Ranter!"

"I'll do my best, sir," said Ben, panting.

Taking a deep breath, Ben began to run. The treadmill went faster and faster. Ben's heart thudded harder. His legs became a blur. The soles of his shoes began to sizzle and steam.

The Treadmill Time Machine whizzed beneath Ben's feet. His legs ached. His head pounded. However, Ben didn't stop. He didn't slow down.

He ran faster. And faster. And even faster still.

At last, the machine bleeped and the treadmill began to slow down. Ben slowed down too.

Now, the control panel on the machine said: THE FUTURE – one term ahead.

Ben stepped off, gasping for breath. He looked around. The Head had vanished. The office was now painted white. There was a black sofa in the corner of the room.

Ben started to get a bad feeling in the pit of his stomach. He opened the door cautiously and peered out into the corridor.

Chapter 2:
The correct uniform

Ben stared around in shock. He almost didn't recognize his own school!

The corridors and floors had been repainted. Little gangs of Ranter's bunny-wunnies patrolled the corridors. All the pupils were dressed in black and white. Even the Hero Academy logo was different!

"You!" A man with blue skin pointed at Ben. "Why aren't you wearing the correct uniform?"

Ben gasped. "Super Coldo! What are you doing here?"

"How dare you talk to a teacher like that?" Super Coldo snarled. "I should put you in the power-drain room as punishment."

Everything had changed.

Super Coldo snapped his fingers and a bunny-wunny hopped up.

"Give this boy a Villain Academy jumper," Super Coldo demanded.

Villain Academy! Ben gulped. Something had gone very, very wrong indeed.

The bunny-wunny opened the hatch in its tummy and pulled out a black jumper. Ben hastily put it on.

"Now stop dawdling and get to assembly," Super Coldo ordered.

Ben lined up for assembly. Maybe one of his friends could explain what had happened. The problem was, he didn't recognize any of the pupils. Where were Pip, Axel and the others?

As they walked into the hall, Ben glanced at the girl behind him.

"What are *you* looking at?" she snarled.

"Good morning, Villain Academy!" boomed a familiar voice.

Ben looked up and gasped. An enormous hologram of Ray Ranter's head appeared from a projector on the stage.

Ranter glared at the pupils. "My bunny-wunnies have reported a 12% increase in villainous behaviour," he said. "As your head teacher, I am very disappointed. It should be double that!"

Ben was speechless. Somehow, Ray Ranter had replaced the Head and taken over the school!

"Get to lessons," Ranter ordered. "And remember our school motto ..."

"Do your worst!" chanted the pupils and teachers.

Ben followed the other pupils to the next lesson. When he got to the classroom, he froze. The teacher was a villain he'd met before … it was Doctor Daze!

Doctor Daze held up her hand for silence. "Today, we are learning how to rob banks by hypnotizing people."

Hesitantly, Ben put up his hand. "Umm, excuse me, please?"

Doctor Daze glared at Ben. "No questions," she snapped. "Questions will get you thrown in the power-drain room!"

Ben gulped and kept quiet for the rest of the lesson.

Ben was glad when lunchtime came. If he could find his friends, they'd be able to help him save the academy.

Mrs Butterworth's eyebrows shot up in surprise when she saw him. "Ben!" she whispered. "How did you get out of the power-drain room?"

Ben frowned. "What's the power-drain room?"

"Oh dear," said Mrs Butterworth. "That room must've drained your memory as well as your powers! It's where Ranter trapped all the heroes when he took over as Head."

"How did Ranter take over?" Ben asked.

Mrs Butterworth looked miserable. "It was my fault. I received an email which said I'd won tickets to my favourite TV show, *Dinner Ladies on Ice*. But when I downloaded the tickets, a computer virus attacked the school supercomputer and made Ray Ranter the new Head." Mrs Butterworth dabbed her eyes. "It was my fault, but I don't know how to save Hero Academy!"

Ben didn't know either. Not yet. However, he did know that he couldn't do it alone. He needed to rescue his friends.

"Tell me how to get to the power-drain room," he said.

"It's in the basement," Mrs Butterworth whispered.

A minute later, Ben skidded to a halt outside the power-drain room. The walls were made out of red glowing energy that acted like a force field, surrounding all of Ben's friends and teachers.

"Ben? Is that you?" Pip's muffled voice came from inside. "Stay back! The walls are made of power-sucking energy!"

"How do I free you?" Ben called.

"You don't!" said a frosty voice behind him.

Ben whirled around, his heart thumping. "Super Coldo!"

"*Ice* try, Ben," said Super Coldo. "But I thought I recognized you earlier. Now I'm going to turn you from hero to *sub-zero*."

Super Coldo fired his ice-blaster at Ben, but Ben was too fast for him. Ben dodged to one side, and the ice hit the power-drain room. The red force field turned blue and shattered into hundreds of shards of ice.

"We're free!" cried Pip.

"And our powers are back," added Axel, testing his invisibility power by making his hand disappear.

"Not for long!" Super Coldo growled, running off. Seconds later, an alarm rang.

Chapter 3:
Wiping the virus

"We need a plan to shut down Ranter's computer virus," Ben said to the group.

Axel scratched his head. "Resetting the school supercomputer might do it. That should wipe the virus and bring the real Head back."

"Brilliant plan, Axel!" Ben high-fived him and Axel blushed.

"Where's the school supercomputer?" Ben asked.

"It's in the data room on the next floor up," Axel replied.

Just then, Super Coldo returned with Doctor Daze and lots of bunny-wunnies. Ray Ranter's head appeared above them.

"You can't win!" Ranter said with a smirk. "There are too many of us!"

"Oh, *really*?" cried a voice behind them all.

Mrs Butterworth and Miss Baker ploughed through the bunny-wunnies, brandishing their rolling pins.

Magnus the caretaker jumped out from a cupboard twirling a mop.

Slink appeared from an air vent as Combat Cat.

"Go, Ben!" Pip cried. "You're the fastest. We'll hold them off!"

Ben dodged past the villains and dashed up to the next floor. Behind him, he heard bashing and crashing sounds as his friends held back the bunny-wunnies.

The data room was stacked with rows and rows of computer towers. Most of them were blue. One of them was glowing red. That had to be the one infected with the virus! Ben sped towards it.

"Wait!" Ranter's hologram head appeared in front of Ben. "Join Villain Academy, Ben. I'll give you full marks in every exam. What do you say?"

"I say ... no!" Ben scowled at the projection. "I think it's time we shut down Villain Academy!"

"DON'T YOU—" Ranter was cut short as Ben switched off the supercomputer. Ranter's hologram head vanished.

Ben reset the supercomputer, then ran back down the stairs.

Had their plan worked?

Ben sprinted back to the power-drain room where he saw all the villains cowering away from an enormous projection of the Head. He was back!

"Reactivating power-drain force field!" said the Head. The red glowing walls suddenly reappeared, but this time they surrounded all the villainous teachers and the bunny-wunnies.

"My freeze-ray isn't working!" yelled Super Coldo.

"We're trapped!" Doctor Daze wailed.

"No," said the Head. "You're *expelled*."

Ben and his friends cheered.

Now Ben had saved the future, he needed to get back to the present. He stayed around just long enough to see Magnus take down the Villain Academy flag and replace it with the Hero Academy one.

Then, as everyone celebrated, he reluctantly sneaked away to the Treadmill Time Machine.

Chapter 4:
Return to the present

Ben stepped on the treadmill. He started to run –
backwards, this time.

"I really hope this works," he thought.

Ben ran as hard and as fast as he could. It felt
strange to be running backwards, but he kept going
until his legs started to ache.

At last, the control panel changed to:
THE PRESENT.

Ben breathed a sigh of relief.

The Head's
office was
back to
normal,
and the
Head was
waiting for
him with Slink.

"My supercomputer brain now predicts a 99% chance that Hero Academy will be safe from Ray Ranter next term," the Head said, smiling. "You did it, Ben!"

Ben smiled back. "We all did," he said. "Teachers, pupils, everyone."

"Spoken like a true hero," the Head replied.

Ben blushed with pride. Then his eyes fell upon the clock, and his jaw dropped.

"Oh no!" he cried. "I missed the final HAT exam!"

"Don't worry," the Head said.

"What do you mean?" asked Ben.

The Head smiled. "The HATs are about showing how far you've come as heroes. With your bravery and determination, you've saved our school. That deserves a pass, don't you think, Slink?"

Slink purred.

"Thank you!" Ben said with a grin.

Ben left the Head's office. He couldn't wait to see his friends! He could hear them all laughing as they celebrated the end of the year. However, before he joined them, he had one final job to do ...

Ben sprinted to the dinner hall. "Mrs Butterworth," he said. "You're going to get an email about winning tickets to see *Dinner Ladies on Ice.*"

Mrs Butterworth's face lit up. "Oooh! My favourite TV show!"

"But it's not real," Ben warned. "Whatever you do, don't open the attachment. It contains a computer virus."

Mrs Butterworth gave a disappointed sigh. "Thank you for the warning, Ben." Then she gave him a strange look. "Wait. How do you know that? Ben? ... Ben!"

Ben rushed outside. Everyone had gathered after the test to celebrate. Ben felt all mixed up with happiness and sadness as he high-fived Axel and joked around with Pip. He would miss them all over the summer, but he'd soon see them again when school restarted.

"I didn't see you at the HAT," Pip said. "Where were you?"

Ben just smiled. "I'll tell you another time, Pip. It's a long story."

"I've had so much fun this year!" Pip said. "I wonder what we'll learn next year?"

"Who knows?" said Axel. "We can't predict the future."

Ben smiled to himself. "Something tells me we'll be just fine." He looked around at all his friends and teachers. "Whatever happens, the world will always need heroes."